Common Core
Reading
Warm-Ups & Test Practice

Newmark Learning
145 Huguenot Street
New Rochelle, NY • 10801

Editor: Ellen Ungaro
Designer: Raquel Hernández
Photo credits: Page 34: Courtesy of US National Archives; Page 54: © Raimond Spekking/CC-BY-SA-3.0 (via Wikimedia Commons); Page 93: TOM VAN DYKE KRT/Newscom

Table of Contents

Contents	Page
Introduction	4
Warm Up 1 Poetry: Sonnet for Morning RL.7.1, RL.7.4, RL.7.5	13
Warm Up 2 Social Studies Text: Preserving the Future RI.7.1, RI.7.2, RI.7.4	17
Warm Up 3 Realistic Fiction: On the Road RL.7.1, RL.7.2, RL.7.3, RL.7.6	22
Warm Up 4 Social Studies Text: The Landscape of Egypt RI.7.1, RI.7.2, RI.7.3, RI.7.5	26
Warm Up 5 Historical Fiction: A New Neighbor RL.7.1, RL.7.3, RL.7.4	30
Warm Up 6 Autobiography: from "The Life of Thomas A. Edison" RI.7.3, RI.7.4, RI.7.6	34
Warm Up 7 Fantasy: Meeting the Scarecrow RL.7.1, RL.7.2, RL.7.3	39
Warm Up 8 Informational Nonfiction: A History-Changing Industry: Movie Making RI.7.1, RI.7.2, RI.7.5, RI.7.8	44
Warm Up 9 Realistic Fiction: Paint Pals RL.7.1, RL.7.3, RL.7.4, RL.7.6	49
Warm Up 10 Opinion: Water Safety RI.7.2, RI.7.4, RI.7.6, RI.7.8	54
Practice Test 1 Realistic Fiction: Helping Hands RL.7.1, RL.7.2, RL.7.3, RL.7.4, RL.7.6	59
Practice Test 2 Social Studies Text: from *The Story of the Pony Express* RI.7.1, RI.7.2, RI.7.3, RI.7.4, RI.7.5, RI.7.6, RI.7.8	69
Practice Test 3 Realistic Fiction: The Land of the Free Poetry: Fireworks RL.7.1, RL.7.2, RL.7.3, RL.7.4, RL.7.6	79
Practice Test 4 Social Studies Text: The Story of Today's Olympics Opinion: Big Changes Since Ancient Greece RI.7.1, RI.7.2, RI.7.3, RI.7.4, RI.7.6, RI.7.8, RI.7.9	91
Answer Key	103

Introduction

What are the new Common Core assessments?

The Common Core State Standards for English Language Arts have set shared, consistent, and clear objectives of what students are expected to learn. The standards are intended to be rigorous and reflect what students will need to be able to do to be college and career ready by the end of high school.

As a part of this initiative, two consortia of states, the Partnership for Assessment of Readiness for College and Careers (PARCC) and Smarter Balanced, have developed new assessments that are aligned with the Common Core State Standards and designed to measure students' progress toward college and career readiness.

How are the new assessments different?

The new standardized assessments from both PARCC and Smarter Balanced are designed to be taken online and include many new types of assessment items.

In addition to multiple-choice questions, the assessments include both short and extended constructed-response questions, which require students to develop written responses that include examples and details from the text.

Another key element in the PARCC and Smarter Balanced assessments is the two-part question. In two-part questions, Part B asks students to identify the text evidence that supports their answer to Part A. These questions reflect the new emphasis on text evidence in the Common Core Standards. Anchor Standard 1 states that students should "cite specific textual evidence when writing or speaking to support conclusions drawn from the text."

The assessments from PARCC and Smarter Balanced also include technology-enhanced questions. These items, which students will encounter if they take the online assessments, ask students to interact with and manipulate text. For example, some questions ask students to select two or three correct answers from a list. Other questions ask students to identify important events in a story and then arrange them in the correct order.

The assessments from PARCC and Smarter Balanced will also feature passages that meet the requirements for complex texts set by the Common Core State Standards. The ability to read and comprehend complex text is another key element of the new standards. Anchor Standard 10 for reading states that students should be able to "Read and comprehend complex literary and informational texts independently and proficiently."

Common Core Reading Warm-Ups & Test Practice is designed to help prepare students for these new assessments from PARCC and Smarter Balanced. The Warm Ups and Practice Tests will help students rehearse the kind of thinking needed for success on the online assessments.

What Test Will Your State Take?

Smarter Balanced States	PARCC States
Alaska	Arizona
California	Arkansas
Connecticut	Colorado
Delaware	District of Columbia
Hawaii	Florida
Idaho	Georgia
Iowa	Illinois
Kansas	Indiana
Maine	Kentucky
Michigan	Louisiana
Missouri	Maryland
Montana	Massachusetts
Nevada	Mississippi
New Hampshire	New Jersey
North Carolina	New Mexico
North Dakota	New York
Oregon	North Dakota
Pennsylvania	Ohio
South Carolina	Oklahoma
South Dakota	Pennsylvania
U.S. Virgin Islands	Rhode Island
Vermont	Tennessee
Washington	
West Virginia	
Wisconsin	
Wyoming	

How will this book help my students prepare for the new assessments?

Warm Ups for Guided Practice

Common Core Reading Warm-Ups and Test Practice include 10 Warm Up tests that are designed to provide students with an opportunity for quick, guided practice.

The 10 Warm Ups feature short reading passages that include examples of the genres that students are required to read and will encounter on the test. In grade 7, the Common Core State Standards require students to read stories, drama, poetry, social studies, science, and technical texts.

Fairy Tale

Poetry

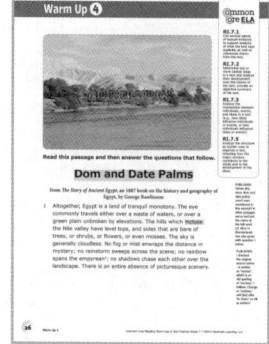

Memoir

Technical/How-to

The questions that follow the Warm Ups include the variety of formats and question types that students will encounter on the new assessments. They include two-part questions, constructed response (short answer) questions, and questions that replicate the technology-enhanced items.

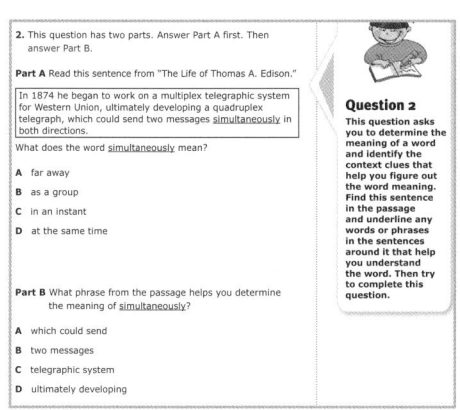

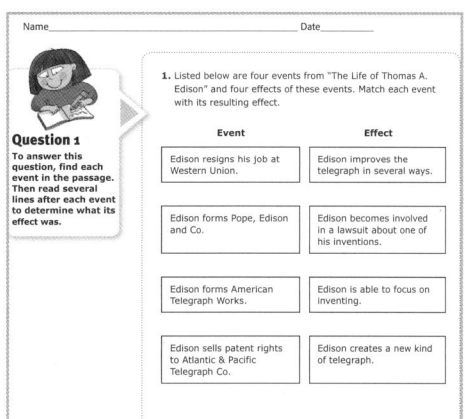

The Warm Ups also include prompts with each question. These prompts provide students with tips and strategies for answering the questions.

Question 1
Reread the poem and look for details that support each statement. If there are no supporting details, you can eliminate the answer choice. For example, in the first stanza, the poet goes out "to wait" for the sunrise. That doesn't support the idea that the poet is impatient.

Question 1
The central ideas in informational text are the big ideas. They are usually referred to more than once in a text. You can eliminate any of the answer choices that are details or only mentioned once.

Question 3
The strongest expression of an author's argument usually occurs at the end of the section, where the author sums up his points and makes the final statement of his claims. Reread the end of paragraph 2 to help you answer this question.

©2014 Newmark Learning, LLC   Common Core Reading Warm-Ups & Test Practice Grade 7

Practice Tests to Build Test-Taking Stamina

The Practice Tests feature longer passages that match the passage lengths that will be used for the PARCC and Smarter Balanced tests. These passages provide students with experience reading the longer and more complex texts they will have to read on the new assessments.

Two of the Practice Tests also feature paired passages. The paired passages give students the opportunity to compare and contrast texts and integrate information from multiple texts, as required by Standard R.9.

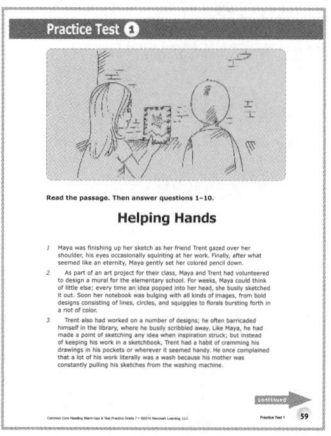

Literature

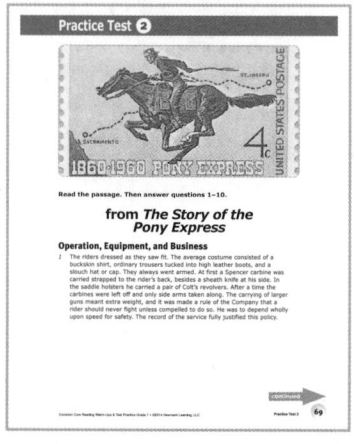

Informational Texts

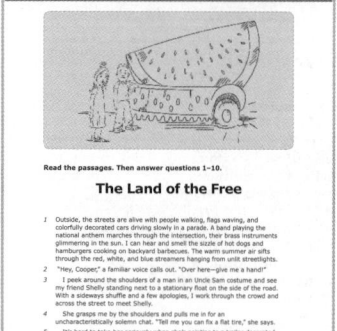

Paired Texts

Each passage is followed by a complete set of questions that reflects the number of questions students will find with each passage on the new assessments. In addition, similar to the Warm Ups, the Practice Tests also include the types of questions students will encounter. Every Practice Test also includes three constructed response (short answer) questions to give students practice writing about texts and using details from the text in their response.

1. This question has two parts. Answer Part A first. Then answer Part B.

   Part A Which sentence **best** describes a theme of the passage?
   - A Working together can result in great things.
   - B It is important to follow through on projects.
   - C Art can be used to solve problems.
   - D Successful projects require organized ideas.

   Part B Which statement from the passage supports the answer to Part A?
   - A For weeks, Maya could think of little else; every time an idea popped into her head, she busily sketched it out.
   - B . . . Trent had a habit of cramming his drawings in his pockets or wherever it seemed handy.
   - C Maya looked at an expectant Trent and said, "Well, you can count me in!"
   - D The wall would truly be filled with color and light—and the energy of everyone who helped.

Two-part questions

6. How does each character contribute to the story's resolution?
   - A Trent excitedly explains the handprint border and Maya finally understands the purpose of his mural.
   - B Maya gets tired of arguing with Trent and agrees to use his mural sketch.
   - C Trent patiently asks Maya questions about her sketch until she realizes her mural will not work.
   - D Trent describes his sketch and Maya realizes he is passionate about his idea.

Questions with multiple answers

8. What is Maya's reaction to Trent's mural idea and how does this reaction affect the plot? Use details from the text to support your answer.

9. Identify the conflict and the theme of the story. How does the conflict help readers understand the theme? Use details from the text to support your answer.

10. Maya and Trent have different ideas about the mural project. How are their ideas alike? How are they different? Use details from the text to support your answer.

Constructed-response questions

Correlated to the Common Core State Standards

All of the assessment items are correlated to the Reading Standards for Literature or the Reading Standards for Informational Text. The chart below shows the standards that each Warm Up and Practice Test addresses.

TEST	RL/RI 7.1	RL/RI 7.2	RL/RI 7.3	RL/RI 7.4	RL/RI 7.5	RL/RI 7.6	RL/RI 7.7	RL/RI 7.8	RL/RI 7.9
Warm Up 1	X			X	X				
Warm Up 2	X	X		X					
Warm Up 3	X	X	X			X			
Warm Up 4	X	X	X		X				
Warm Up 5	X		X	X					
Warm Up 6			X	X		X			
Warm Up 7	X	X	X						
Warm Up 8	X	X			X			X	
Warm Up 9	X		X	X		X			
Warm Up 10		X		X		X		X	
Practice Test 1	X	X	X	X		X			
Practice Test 2	X	X	X	X	X	X		X	
Practice Test 3	X	X	X	X		X			
Practice Test 4	X	X	X	X		X		X	X

Grade 7 Common Core State Standards

Reading Standards for Literature

RL.7.1 Cite several pieces of textual evidence to support analysis of what the text says explicitly as well as inferences drawn from the text.
RL.7.2 Determine a theme or central idea of a text and analyze its development over the course of the text; provide an objective summary of the text.
RL.7.3 Analyze how particular elements of a story or drama interact (e.g., how setting shapes the characters or plot).
RL.7.4 Determine the meaning of words and phrases as they are used in a text, including figurative and connotative meanings; analyze the impact of rhymes and other repetitions of sounds (e.g., alliteration) on a specific verse or stanza of a poem or section of a story or drama.
RL.7.5 Analyze how a drama's or poem's form or structure (e.g., soliloquy, sonnet) contributes to its meaning.
RL.7.6 Analyze how an author develops and contrasts the points of view of different characters or narrators in a text.
RL.7.7 Compare and contrast a written story, drama, or poem to its audio, filmed, staged, or multimedia version, analyzing the effects of techniques unique to each medium (e.g., lighting, sound, color, or camera focus and angles in a film).
RL.7.9 Compare and contrast a fictional portrayal of a time, place, or character and a historical account of the same period as a means of understanding how authors of fiction use or alter history.

Reading Standards for Informational Texts

RI.7.1 Cite several pieces of textual evidence to support analysis of what the text says explicitly as well as inferences drawn from the text.
RI.7.2 Determine two or more central ideas in a text and analyze their development over the course of the text; provide an objective summary of the text.
RI.7.3 Analyze the interactions between individuals, events, and ideas in a text (e.g., how ideas influence individuals or events, or how individuals influence ideas or events).
RI.7.4 Determine the meaning of words and phrases as they are used in a text, including figurative, connotative, and technical meanings; analyze the impact of a specific word choice on meaning and tone.
RI.7.5 Analyze the structure an author uses to organize a text, including how the major sections contribute to the whole and to the development of the ideas.
RI.7.6 Determine an author's point of view or purpose in a text and analyze how the author distinguishes his or her position from that of others.
RI.7.7 Compare and contrast a text to an audio, video, or multimedia version of the text, analyzing each medium's portrayal of the subject (e.g., how the delivery of a speech affects the impact of the words).
RI.7.8 Trace and evaluate the argument and specific claims in a text, assessing whether the reasoning is sound and the evidence is relevant and sufficient to support the claims.
RI.7.9 Analyze how two or more authors writing about the same topic shape their presentations of key information by emphasizing different evidence or advancing different interpretations of facts.

How to Use Common Core Reading Warm Ups and Practice Tests

The Warm Ups are designed to be quick and easy practice for students. They can be used in a variety of ways:

- Assign Warm Ups for homework.

- Use them for quick review in class.

- Use them for targeted review of key standards. The correlation chart on page 10 can help identify Warm Ups that address the skills you want to focus on.

The longer Practice Tests can be used to prepare students in the weeks before the assessments. They can also be used to help assess students, reading comprehension throughout the year.

Tear-out Answer Keys

Find the answers to all the Warm Ups and Practice Tests in the Answer Key beginning on page 103. The Answer Key includes the standards correlations for each question. In addition, it includes sample answers for the constructed response (short answer) questions.

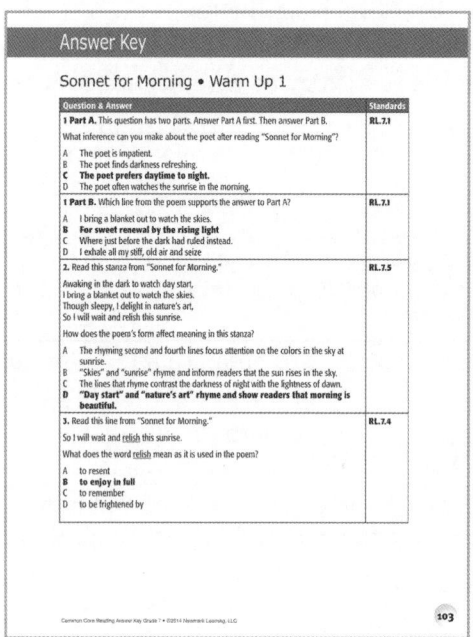

Warm Up 1

Read this passage and then answer the questions that follow.

Sonnet for Morning

1   Awaking in the dark to watch day start,
       I bring a blanket out to watch the skies.
       Though sleepy, I delight in nature's art,
       So I will wait and relish this sunrise.

5   It comes: the cold and gray of morning fades,
       And passion's colors—pink, red, orange—spread.
       Across the city, newest light invades
       Where just before the dark had ruled instead.

Common Core ELA Standards

RL.7.1 Cite several pieces of textual evidence to support analysis of what the text says explicitly as well as inferences drawn from the text.

RL.7.4 Determine the meaning of words and phrases as they are used in a text, including figurative and connotative meanings; analyze the impact of rhymes and other repetitions of sounds (e.g., alliteration) on a specific verse or stanza of a poem or section of a story or drama.

RL.7.5 Analyze how a drama's or poem's form or structure (e.g., soliloquy, sonnet) contributes to its meaning.

continued

Warm Up 1 • Sonnet for Morning

The smell of morning flies in with the breeze,
10 Of jasmine petals, cinnamon, and dew.
I exhale all my stiff, old air and seize
The freshest morning breaths, and so can you:
   For sweet renewal by the rising light
   Just wake up early, and exhale the night.

Warm Up 1 • Sonnet for Morning

Name_____ Date_____

1. This question has two parts. Answer Part A first. Then answer Part B.

Part A What inference can you make about the poet after reading "Sonnet for Morning"?

A The poet is impatient.

B The poet finds darkness refreshing.

C The poet prefers daytime to night.

D The poet often watches the sunrise in the morning.

Part B Which line from the poem supports the answer to part A?

A I bring a blanket out to watch the skies.

B For sweet renewal by the rising light

C Where just before the dark had ruled instead.

D I exhale all my stiff, old air and seize

Question 1

Reread the poem and look for details that support each statement. If there are no supporting details, you can eliminate the answer choice. For example, in the first stanza, the poet goes out "to wait" for the sunrise. That doesn't support the idea that the poet is impatient.

continued

Warm Up 1 • Sonnet for Morning

Name_____ Date_____

Question 2
Notice that this poem's form includes rhyme. Poets use rhyme to focus readers' attention on those words. Underline the words that rhyme in this stanza and ask yourself what message the poet is trying to give readers through those words.

2. Read this stanza from "Sonnet for Morning."

> Awaking in the dark to watch day start,
> I bring a blanket out to watch the skies.
> Though sleepy, I delight in nature's art,
> So I will wait and relish this sunrise.

How does the poem's form affect meaning in this stanza?

A The rhyming second and fourth lines focus attention on the colors in the sky at sunrise.

B "Skies" and "sunrise" rhyme and inform readers that the sun rises in the sky.

C The lines that rhyme contrast the darkness of night with the lightness of dawn.

D "Day start" and "nature's art" rhyme and show readers that morning is beautiful.

Question 3
Context clues can help readers determine the meanings of words and phrases. Read the lines around *relish* and look for clues about its meaning. The phrase "delight in nature's art" is one clue to the meaning of the word.

3. Read this line from "Sonnet for Morning."

> So I will wait and relish this sunrise.

What does the word *relish* mean as it is used in the poem?

A to resent

B to enjoy in full

C to remember

D to be frightened by

Warm Up 2

RI.7.1
Cite several pieces of textual evidence to support analysis of what the text says explicitly as well as inferences drawn from the text.

RI.7.2
Determine two or more central ideas in a text and analyze their development over the course of the text; provide an objective summary of the text.

RI.7.4
Determine the meaning of words and phrases as they are used in a text, including figurative, connotative, and technical meanings; analyze the impact of a specific word choice on meaning and tone.

Read this passage and then answer the questions that follow.

Preserving the Future

1 Myths about the Yellowstone region circulated by word of mouth throughout the 1800s—tall tales about bubbling mud and water shooting up from the ground. During a government-funded expedition of the area, a geologist named Ferdinand Hayden uncovered the truth: the stories were real. There were petrified forests, hot springs, and a geyser that would later be called "Old Faithful." Hayden's subsequent report to Congress was important from not only an environmental perspective, but a historical one as well. Convinced that the land was too significant to sell for private use, Congress decided to set it aside for the public to visit.

continued

Warm Up 2 • Preserving the Future

2 On March 1, 1872, Yellowstone became the first national park in the United States. By the time the National Park Service was founded in 1916, there were already thirty-five parks and monuments in existence. Today the National Park Service is responsible for nearly 400 areas that are as diverse as the country we live in. Dry Tortugas National Park, for example, is a former military base on an island south of Florida that can be reached only by plane or boat. On the other side of the country lies Denali National Park in Alaska. Denali contains six million acres of land, including Mount McKinley, which is the tallest point in North America. Even the Golden Gate Bridge in San Francisco is a National Recreational Area.

3 The impetus that began with Yellowstone set off a worldwide effort to preserve environmental and historical landmarks. Currently, there are approximately 1,200 national parks that are maintained by over 100 countries. As a consequence of the steps that were taken to conserve Yellowstone's beauty, geological landscapes and other attractions around the world will continue to exist for future generations to enjoy.

Warm Up 2 • Preserving the Future

Name_____ Date_____

1. This question has two parts. Answer Part A first. Then answer Part B.

Part A Which of the following inferences can you make from the passage?

A The National Park Service requires that all national parks include recreational areas.

B Hot springs are dangerous and must be controlled by the government.

C The National Park Service cares for sites with rare and significant features.

D Geologists determine whether sites should be designated as national parks.

Part B Which detail from the text supports the answer to Part A?

A Even the Golden Gate Bridge in San Francisco is a National Recreational Area.

B On March 1, 1872, Yellowstone became the first national park in the United States.

C The impetus that began with Yellowstone set off a worldwide effort to preserve environmental and historical landmarks.

D During a government-funded expedition of the area, a geologist named Ferdinand Hayden uncovered the truth: the stories were real.

Question 1

The first part of this question asks you to identify an inference that can be made from the text, and the second part asks you to identify a detail from the text that supports that evidence. Before selecting your answer from Part A, make sure that there is a detail in Part B that supports it.

continued

Warm Up 2 • Preserving the Future

Name_____ Date_____

Question 2

A summary tells the most important parts of a story. It leaves out minor details and personal opinions. Place an X next to any of the statements on the list that are minor details or opinions. Then figure out the correct order for the remaining statements.

2. Choose five statements that belong in a summary of "Preserving the Future" and number them in the correct order.

___ There is a geyser in Yellowstone named "Old Faithful."

___ The National Park Service was founded.

___ The government decided Yellowstone was too important to be privately owned and turned it into the first national park.

___ Denali National Park has better geological features than Yellowstone does.

___ Ferdinand Hayden found that there really were petrified forests, hot springs, and a geyser in the Yellowstone area.

___ Visitors must reach Dry Tortugas National Park by boat or plane.

___ There are almost 400 national parks in the United States and 1,200 around the world today.

___ It is important to preserve historic sites for future generations to learn from.

___ In the 1800s, people told wild stories about bubbling mud in the area around Yellowstone.

Warm Up 2 • Preserving the Future

Name_____ Date_____

3. Read this sentence from "Preserving the Future."

> Convinced that the land was too significant to sell for private use, Congress decided to <u>set it aside</u> for the public to visit.

What is the meaning of the phrase <u>set it aside</u> as it is used in this sentence?

A discard it

B contain it within fencing

C prevent it from being enjoyed

D reserve it for a special purpose

Question 3

Read the sentence again, replacing *set it aside* with each answer choice. Ask yourself if the sentence still makes sense. If it does not, you can eliminate that answer choice.

Warm Up 3

Read this passage and then answer the questions that follow.

On the Road

1. "Pack up, kids! We leave tomorrow at dawn!" announced Mr. D'Angelo. All three D'Angelo children knew what that meant: it was time for their annual three-day road trip to visit relatives across the country.

2. Gina, who was thirteen, dreaded the thought of being cramped in the crowded car with her parents and younger brother and sister—and all their luggage and belongings, besides the five bodies. It was going to be a rough ride.

3. "I'm going to pack right now!" shouted Dominic, racing up the stairs to his bedroom and slamming the door shut.

4. Mrs. D'Angelo shook her head and followed, saying, "I had better go help him. Last year he packed only one sandal."

5	Gina decided to leave her packing until the last minute, anticipating the imminent flurry of activity. Instead, she retreated to her favorite spot in the backyard under the willow tree and sprawled out on the cool, spiky grass. Milton, the family cat, approached, sensing an opportunity for some leisurely stroking, and Gina obliged.

6	"Milton, don't you agree that as a teenager I am much too sophisticated now for these trips?" Gina lamented to her silent buddy. "All the girls are going swimming and having sleepovers, and I am going to be stuck with Grandma and Cousin Todd," she groused, discouraged at the thought of missing out on all the fun.

7	The next morning, at the crack of dawn, Gina begrudgingly joined her family as they sleepily loaded themselves into the car and drove away. Gina moped and looked out the window; yet soon she marveled at the sunrise, watching the grand, golden sphere rise slowly above the horizon. Gina chuckled, remembering her father's admonishment to look out the window and enjoy the scenic ride from time to time, and her spirits lifted a bit.

continued

Warm Up 3 • On the Road

Name_____ Date_____

Question 1

A theme is what the story is mostly about. It is sometimes a big idea an author is trying to communicate. Look at each answer choice and ask yourself if it describes what the story is mostly about.

1. This question has two parts. Answer Part A first. Then answer Part B.

Part A What is a theme of "On the Road"?

A Taking a family trip can be enjoyable.

B Young children need help packing for a trip.

C It is important to begin a road trip early in the morning.

D Teenagers would rather spend time with friends than family.

Part B Which detail from the text supports the answer to part A?

A "We leave tomorrow at dawn!" announced Mr. D'Angelo.

B Mrs. D'Angelo shook her head and followed, saying, "I had better go help him."

C "All the girls are going swimming and having sleepovers, and I am going to be stuck with Grandma and Cousin Todd."

D Gina chuckled, remembering her father's admonishment to look out the window and enjoy the scenic ride from time to time, and her spirits lifted a bit.

Warm Up 3 • On the Road

Name_____ Date_____

2. Read this sentence from "On the Road."

> "I'm going to pack right now!" shouted Dominic, racing up the stairs to his bedroom and slamming the door shut.

What does this sentence tell readers about Dominic?

A   He is always in a hurry.

B   He often has temper tantrums.

C   He is excited to pack for the trip.

D   He prefers privacy while he packs.

Question 2

Each answer choice could explain why Dominic ran upstairs and slammed the door. Ask yourself if there is evidence in the text to support each choice. For example, is there a detail that describes Dominic's temper tantrums? If not, you can eliminate it as an answer choice.

3. Which of the following details from the text support the idea that Gina does not want to go on the trip? Check the box next to each detail you choose.

☐   dreaded the thought

☐   slamming the door shut

☐   anticipating the imminent flurry of activity

☐   she groused

☐   sprawled out on the cool, spiky grass

☐   Gina moped and looked out the window

☐   her spirits lifted a bit

Question 3

Authors often use descriptive language to show a character's point of view. For example, compare "'I'll go,' Nathan yelled as he sprinted to the door" and "'I'll go,' Nathan whispered, looking down at the ground." The descriptive language is a clue to what a character is thinking and feeling. Reread "On the Road" to find descriptive words that reflect Gina's point of view.

Warm Up 4

Read this passage and then answer the questions that follow.

The Landscape of Egypt

from *The Story of Ancient Egypt*, an 1887 book on the history and geography of Egypt, by George Rawlinson

1. Altogether, Egypt is a land of tranquil monotony. The eye commonly travels either over a waste of waters, or over a green plain unbroken by elevations. The hills which enclose the Nile valley have level tops, and sides that are bare of trees, or shrubs, or flowers, or even mosses. The sky is generally cloudless. No fog or mist enwraps the distance in mystery; no rainstorm sweeps across the scene; no rainbow spans the empyrean[1]; no shadows chase each other over the landscape. There is an entire absence of picturesque scenery.

[1] The heavens.

A single broad river, unbroken within the limits of Egypt even by a rapid, two flat strips of green plain at its side, two low lines of straight-topped hills beyond them, and a boundless open space where the river divides itself into half a dozen sluggish branches before reaching the sea, constitute Egypt, which is by nature a southern Holland—"weary, stale, flat and unprofitable."

2   The monotony is relieved, however, in two ways, and by two causes. Nature herself does something to relieve it. Twice a day, in the morning and in the evening, the sky and the landscape are lit up by hues so bright yet so delicate, that the homely features of the prospect are at once transformed as by magic, and wear an aspect of exquisite beauty. At dawn long streaks of rosy light stretch themselves across the eastern sky, the haze above the western horizon blushes a deep red; a ruddy light diffuses itself around, and makes walls and towers and minarets and cupolas to glow like fire; the long shadows thrown by each tree and building are purple or violet. A glamour is over the scene, which seems transfigured by an enchanter's wand; but the enchanter is Nature, and the wand she wields is composed of sun-rays.

continued

Warm Up 4 • The Landscape of Egypt

Name_____ Date_____

Question 1

The central ideas in informational text are the big ideas. They are usually referred to more than once in a text. You can eliminate any of the answer choices that are details or only mentioned once.

1. Which of these sentences states a central idea in the passage? Check the box next to each statement you choose.

   ☐ A river flows through the middle of Egypt.
   ☐ Egypt becomes beautiful at sunrise and sunset.
   ☐ Rainstorms do not usually occur in Egypt.
   ☐ The eastern sky turns pink in the morning.
   ☐ The hills in the Nile valley are flat and treeless.
   ☐ The geography of Egypt is plain and uninteresting.
   ☐ The Nile River branches off as it reaches the sea.
   ☐ Egypt is known as the "southern Holland."

Question 2

Read the passage again and draw a line where the topic changes. Ask yourself what the focus is before the line, and what it shifts to after the line.

2. How does the author organize the information provided in the text?

   A The first part describes Egypt's hills and the second part describes the river valley.

   B The first half describes Egypt's monotony and the second half describes its beauty.

   C The first half describes Egypt's geography and the second half describes its history.

   D The first part describes Egypt in the morning and the second part describes it in the evening.

Warm Up 4 • The Landscape of Egypt

Name_____ Date_____

3. This question has two parts. Answer Part A first. Then answer Part B.

Part A Read this sentence from the passage.

> Nature herself does something to relieve it.

What does nature relieve in this passage?

A the stillness of the Nile River

B the monotony of Egypt's landscape

C the drought across the Nile valley

D the extreme temperatures across Egypt

Question 3

Find this sentence in the passage and underline it. Read the sentences around it and underline the details in the text that show what nature relieves.

Part B Which detail from the text supports the answer to Part A?

A The sky is generally cloudless.

B A glamour is over the scene which seems transfigured by an enchanter's wand.

C The hills which enclose the Nile valley have level tops, and sides that are bare of trees, or shrubs, or flowers, or even mosses.

D No shadows chase each other over the landscape.

Warm Up 5

Read this passage and then answer the questions that follow.

A New Neighbor

1   "Beth," my sister calls from outside, "the new neighbors have arrived!"

2   I race downstairs and join my sister on the front porch. There has been a lot of talk about the family and I am very curious to actually meet them. The family is moving in with the Swensons, an older couple who have extra space to share with those in need. Our papa says some of our neighbors are complaining about the Swensons, but I wish we had room to share, too.

3   "They're already indoors; they didn't have much with them," my sister says. "Mrs. Swenson said that it took them weeks to get here from Georgia."

4   The War Between the States has been raging for what seems like ages, and from our home in Boston we hear constant news about the fighting. In the past few months, many former slaves have made their way to our neighborhood after leaving the South. Some families, like the Swensons, have been giving them places to stay to help them begin a new life here.

5   "Are there children in the family?" I ask my sister.

6   She says she saw a boy about my age, and I'm a little disappointed because I was hoping for a girl my age. My sister and I go back into the house, and it's not until the next day that I get to meet him. I see him sitting on the steps outside the Swensons' home.

7   "Hello!" I shout, as I walk toward him. He looks at me cautiously as I approach, so I introduce myself and ask him to be my friend.

8   "I'm Pete," he replies, still seeming uncomfortable. I consider retreating—perhaps he won't want to be my friend—but I am too curious to hear his story to give up yet. Despite his tired-looking face and the hard life I can only imagine he's endured, Pete suddenly smiles at me.

9   "I guess I could use a friend," he says.

10 "So could I," I answer as I join him on the steps.

continued

Warm Up 5 • A New Neighbor

Name_____ Date_____

Question 1

Inferences are based on evidence in the text. Read each answer choice and ask yourself: Does this support the idea that the family moving into the Swensons' house is controversial?

1. Which of the following details from the passage support the inference that the family moving into the Swensons' house is controversial? Check the box next to each statement you choose.

   ☐ I am very curious to actually meet them
   ☐ some of our neighbors are complaining
   ☐ we hear constant news about the fighting
   ☐ There has been a lot of talk about the family
   ☐ it took them weeks to get here from Georgia
   ☐ He looks at me cautiously as I approach

Question 2

When you come across a word that you don't know, looking at the root words, prefixes, and suffixes can help you. The root word in this example is *retreat*. The prefix *re-* means back or again.

2. Read this sentence from "A New Neighbor."

   > I consider <u>retreating</u>—perhaps he won't want to be my friend—but I am too curious to hear his story to give up yet.

   What does the word <u>retreating</u> mean?

   A going over one's route again

   B taking back something that was said

   C backing away from someone or something

   D drawing together to make smaller

Warm Up 5 • A New Neighbor

Name_____ Date_____

3. Choose a trait to describe each character in the story. Write the letter next to the character's name in the Trait column. Then choose an action that reveals the trait. Write the letter next to the character's name in the Action column.

Character	Trait	Action
Beth's sister		
Beth		
Pete		
The Swensons		

Traits	Actions
A wary	**H** introduces herself to a new neighbor
B unkind	**I** reads about President Lincoln
C observant	**J** shares extra space with former slaves
D jealous	**K** notices the new neighbors do not have many belongings
E sympathetic	**L** fights in the War Between the States
F impatient	**M** shouts at family members
G outgoing	**N** watches carefully as others approach

Question 3
Reread the passage and look for each action. If you cannot find an action in the passage, cross it off the list. When you find an action, determine who performs it and write the letter for that action in the correct character's row. Once you have matched the characters with their actions, you can identify the trait that fits the best.

Warm Up 6

Read this passage and answer the questions that follow.

from "The Life of Thomas A. Edison"

from Inventing Entertainment, Motion Pictures and Sound Recordings of the Edison Companies by the Library of Congress

1   In 1868 Edison moved to Boston, where he worked in the Western Union office and worked even more on his inventions. In January 1869 Edison resigned his job, intending to devote himself fulltime to inventing things. His first invention to receive a patent was the electric vote recorder, in June 1869.

2 During the next period of his life, Edison became involved in multiple projects and partnerships dealing with the telegraph. In October 1869 Edison formed with Franklin L. Pope and James Ashley the organization Pope, Edison and Co. They advertised themselves as electrical engineers and constructors of electrical devices. Edison received several patents for improvements to the telegraph. The partnership merged with the Gold and Stock Telegraph Co. in 1870. Edison also established the Newark Telegraph Works in Newark, New Jersey, with William Unger to manufacture stock printers. He formed the American Telegraph Works to work on developing an automatic telegraph later in the year. In 1874 he began to work on a multiplex telegraphic system for Western Union, ultimately developing a quadruplex telegraph, which could send two messages simultaneously in both directions. When Edison sold his patent rights to the quadruplex to the rival Atlantic & Pacific Telegraph Co., a series of court battles followed in which Western Union won. Besides other telegraph inventions, he also developed an electric pen in 1875.

3 Edison opened a new laboratory in Menlo Park, New Jersey, in 1876. This site later become known as an "invention factory," since they worked on several different inventions at any given time there. Edison would conduct numerous experiments to find answers to problems. He said, "I never quit until I get what I'm after. Negative results are just what I'm after. They are just as valuable to me as positive results."

Warm Up 6 • from "The Life of Thomas A. Edison"

Name_____ Date_____

Question 1

To answer this question, find each event in the passage. Then read several lines after each event to determine what its effect was.

1. Listed below are four events from "The Life of Thomas A. Edison" and four effects of these events. Match each event with its resulting effect.

Event	Effect
Edison resigns his job at Western Union.	Edison improves the telegraph in several ways.
Edison forms Pope, Edison and Co.	Edison becomes involved in a lawsuit about one of his inventions.
Edison forms American Telegraph Works.	Edison is able to focus on inventing.
Edison sells patent rights to Atlantic & Pacific Telegraph Co.	Edison creates a new kind of telegraph.

Warm Up 6 • from "The Life of Thomas A. Edison"

Name_____ Date_____

2. This question has two parts. Answer Part A first. Then answer Part B.

Part A Read this sentence from "The Life of Thomas A. Edison."

> In 1874 he began to work on a multiplex telegraphic system for Western Union, ultimately developing a quadruplex telegraph, which could send two messages simultaneously in both directions.

What does the word simultaneously mean?

A far away

B as a group

C in an instant

D at the same time

Part B What phrase from the passage helps you determine the meaning of simultaneously?

A which could send

B two messages

C telegraphic system

D ultimately developing

Question 2

This question asks you to determine the meaning of a word and identify the context clues that help you figure out the word meaning. Find this sentence in the passage and underline any words or phrases in the sentences around it that help you understand the word. Then try to complete this question.

continued

Warm Up 6 • from "The Life of Thomas A. Edison"

Name_____ Date_____

Question 3

Think about the type of information the author included in the passage. Did the author include details about why Edison invented an electric vote recorder? Is there information about how people used his inventions? Answering these questions will help you identify the author's purpose.

Question 4

To answer this question, think about what a factory is like. What qualities does a factory have?

3. What is the author's purpose in "The Life of Thomas A. Edison"?

A to discuss the effects of some of Edison's inventions

B to explain the reasons why Edison created his inventions

C to provide a time line of Edison's development as an inventor

D to prove that Edison was an important and successful inventor

4. Why do you think Edison's laboratory became known as an "invention factory"? Use details from the passage to support your answer.

_____

_____

_____

_____

_____

_____

_____

_____

Warm Up 7

Read this passage and then answer the questions that follow.

Meeting the Scarecrow

by L. Frank Baum, from *The Wizard of Oz*

1 After being caught in a tornado, Dorothy finds herself in a strange land called Oz. She is following a path called the Yellow Brick Road in order to find the wizard who can help her get home.

2 She bade her friends good-bye, and again started along the road of yellow brick. When she had gone several miles she thought she would stop to rest, and so climbed to the top of the fence beside the road and sat down. There was a great cornfield beyond the fence, and not far away she saw a Scarecrow, placed high on a pole to keep the birds from the ripe corn.

3 Dorothy leaned her chin upon her hand and gazed thoughtfully at the Scarecrow. Its head was a small sack stuffed with straw, with eyes, nose, and mouth painted on it to represent a face. An old, pointed blue hat, that had belonged to some Munchkin, was perched on his head, and the rest of the figure was a blue suit of clothes, worn and faded, which had also been stuffed with straw. On the feet were some old boots with blue tops, such as every man wore in this country, and the figure was raised above the stalks of corn by means of the pole stuck up its back.

Common Core ELA Standards

RL.7.1 Cite several pieces of textual evidence to support analysis of what the text says explicitly as well as inferences drawn from the text.

RL.7.2 Determine a theme or central idea of a text and analyze its development over the course of the text; provide an objective summary of the text.

RL.7.3 Analyze how particular elements of a story or drama interact (e.g., how setting shapes the characters or plot).

continued

Warm Up 7 • Meeting the Scarecrow

4   While Dorothy was looking earnestly into the queer, painted face of the Scarecrow, she was surprised to see one of the eyes slowly wink at her. She thought she must have been mistaken at first, for none of the scarecrows in Kansas ever wink; but presently the figure nodded its head to her in a friendly way. Then she climbed down from the fence and walked up to it, while Toto ran around the pole and barked.

5   "Good day," said the Scarecrow, in a rather husky voice.

6   "Did you speak?" asked the girl, in wonder.

7   "Certainly," answered the Scarecrow. "How do you do?"

8   "I'm pretty well, thank you," replied Dorothy politely. "How do you do?"

9   "I'm not feeling well," said the Scarecrow, with a smile, "for it is very tedious being perched up here night and day to scare away crows."

10   "Can't you get down?" asked Dorothy.

11   "No, for this pole is stuck up my back. If you will please take away the pole I shall be greatly obliged to you."

12   Dorothy reached up both arms and lifted the figure off the pole, for, being stuffed with straw, it was quite light.

13   "Thank you very much," said the Scarecrow, when he had been set down on the ground. "I feel like a new man."

Warm Up 7 • Meeting the Scarecrow

Name_____ Date_____

1. Which of the following details from the passage tell the reader that the setting of the story is unusual? Place a check in the box next to each detail you choose.

   ❑ There was a great cornfield beyond the fence.

   ❑ Its head was a small sack stuffed with straw, with eyes, nose, and mouth painted on it to represent a face.

   ❑ On the feet were some old boots with blue tops, such as every man wore in this country,

   ❑ An old, pointed blue hat, that had belonged to some Munchkin, was perched on his head.

   ❑ She thought she must have been mistaken at first, for none of the scarecrows in Kansas ever wink.

   ❑ "Did you speak?" asked the girl, in wonder.

   ❑ "Thank you very much," said the Scarecrow, when he had been set down on the ground.

Question 1

A story's setting is an important part of the story. In this case, the details about the setting tell the reader that the story is most likely a fantasy because things happen in the story that cannot happen in real life.

continued

Warm Up 7 • Meeting the Scarecrow

Name_____ Date_____

Question 2

To make an inference about a character, look at what they say and what they do. What does Dorothy do when she first sees the scarecrow? What does she say?

2. This question has two parts. Answer Part A first. Then answer Part B.

Part A What inference can you make about Dorothy in "Meeting the Scarecrow"?

A She is brave.

B She is lonely.

C She is stubborn.

D She is intelligent.

Part B What detail from the passage helps you make this inference?

A Dorothy leaned her chin upon her hand and gazed thoughtfully at the Scarecrow.

B She thought she must have been mistaken at first, for none of the scarecrows in Kansas ever wink.

C Then she climbed down from the fence and walked up to it, while Toto ran around the pole and barked.

D While Dorothy was looking earnestly into the queer, painted face of the Scarecrow, she was surprised to see one of the eyes slowly wink at her.

Warm Up 7 • Meeting the Scarecrow

Name_____ Date_____

3. Choose four sentences that should be included in a summary of this passage and number them in the correct order.

___ Dorothy and the Scarecrow greet each other.

___ Dorothy is walking down the yellow brick road.

___ The scarecrow surprises Dorothy by winking at her.

___ The scarecrow is wearing worn and old clothing and old blue boots.

___ Dorothy helps the scarecrow by taking him down from a pole.

___ Toto is afraid of the scarecrow and barks at him.

___ Dorothy is sitting on a fence in a cornfield.

___ Dorothy stops to rest in a cornfield and sees a scarecrow.

___ Dorothy is able to pick up the scarecrow because he is very light.

___ Dorothy is kind and polite to the scarecrow.

Question 3

Remember that a summary should include only the major events that happen in a story. It should not include minor details or events that happen before or after the story's action. A summary should also not include any personal opinions or inferences.

Warm Up 8

Common Core ELA Standards

RI.7.1 Cite several pieces of textual evidence to support analysis of what the text says explicitly as well as inferences drawn from the text.

RI.7.2 Determine a theme or central idea of a text and analyze its development over the course of the text; provide an objective summary of the text.

RI.7.5 Analyze the structure an author uses to organize a text, including how the major sections contribute to the whole and to the development of the ideas.

RI.7.8 Trace and evaluate the argument and specific claims in a text, assessing whether the reasoning is sound and the evidence is relevant and sufficient to support the claims.

In 1878, photographer Eadward Muybridge took a series of photographs that, when viewed in sequence, show a horse running. Many people believe it was the first step in making motion pictures.

Read this passage and answer the questions that follow.

A History-Changing Industry: Movie Making

1   Filmmaking, or cinematography, began and developed with startling rapidity, spreading throughout the modern world in a few short decades. Near the close of the nineteenth century, photography, though still a recent invention, underwent quick advancement. As camera makers crafted devices that could shoot multiple photographs per second, other inventors got creative: they played with the idea of stringing photographs together to form "moving" pictures. Just before the turn of the twentieth century, Thomas Edison publicized a moving-picture contraption that began what would be perhaps the most prosperous and culturally impactful industry of our time: the movie industry.

Warm Up 8 • A History-Changing Industry: Movie Making

2   Edison's idea spread quickly. Within ten years, moving pictures were being produced and shown across America in theaters called nickelodeons; admission usually cost five cents. Movies met comparable popularity in Europe. The first films were silent, with colorless images that today's film watchers might consider blurry.

3   Around the 1930s, movies with sound—then popularly referred to as "talkies"—spread like wildfire. By implementing dialogue and music, filmmakers could utilize another realm of creativity.

4   As films developed through special effects, actor training, and plot complexity, they gained cultural influence. During the time of the Great Depression and World War II, films with uplifting messages sought to spread hope among the downhearted American people. In later decades, movies continued that cultural commentary. They helped to shape ideas about things like childhood, family, and the good life; and they raised questions about things people feared and imagined about history, science, human nature, and the future.

5   The film industry continues to impact society and generate large amounts of revenue. Cinematography persists as both art and entertainment to viewers, often delighting, surprising, and challenging people. There will always be good movies and less-than-good movies, but all of them contribute to and preserve invaluable snapshots of history in their makeup and in the stories they tell.

continued

Warm Up 8 • A History-Changing Industry: Movie Making

Name_____ Date_____

Question 1

Remember that an inference must be based on a factual detail from the passage. If you cannot find a detail in the passage that provides support for one of the answer choices, that answer choice cannot be the correct inference.

1. This question has two parts. Answer Part A first. Then answer Part B.

Part A What inference can be made about movie viewers from the information in "A History-Changing Industry: Movie Making"?

A Most viewers like to watch movies that are about topics that challenge them.

B Most viewers were not really interested in movies until the introduction of sound.

C Movie viewers today expect movies with better visual quality than did viewers of long ago.

D Movie viewers today are willing to sacrifice plot complexity for improved special effects.

Part B Which detail from the passage helps you draw this inference?

A The first films were silent, with colorless images that today's film watchers might consider blurry.

B As films developed through special effects, actor training, and plot complexity, they gained cultural influence.

C Cinematography persists as both art and entertainment to viewers, often delighting, surprising, and challenging people.

D As camera makers crafted devices that could shoot multiple photographs per second, other inventors got creative: they played with the idea of stringing photographs together to form "moving" pictures.

Warm Up 8 • A History-Changing Industry: Movie Making

Name_____ Date_____

2. Which structure does the author use to organize "A History-Changing Industry: Movie Making"?

A cause/effect

B chronological

C compare/contrast

D problem/solution

3. Read the statements below about "A History-Changing Industry: Movie Making." Check the box next to each statement that is a central idea in the passage.

☐ Each culture has its own particular style of movies.

☐ Movies developed and spread quickly throughout society.

☐ Special effects helped movies become more popular.

☐ Early movies were silent and filmed in black and white.

☐ Movies both influence and reflect the times in which they are made.

Question 2
Structure is the way the information in a passage is organized. To determine a passage's structure, pay attention to the way each paragraph relates to the paragraph before it. You can also look for signal words that tell you the text structure. For example, *since* and *as a result of* can signal cause/effect, while time words can signal chronological order.

Question 3
Remember that a central idea is an idea that is developed in at least one paragraph of the passage. An idea that is discussed in a sentence or two is a supporting detail, not a central idea.

continued

Warm Up 8 • A History-Changing Industry: Movie Making

Name_____ Date_____

Question 4

Reread the passage and underline any statements that show the author's opinion. Review all of the statements together to determine the author's point of view.

4. What is the author's point of view about the impact of movies? What information does the author use to support this point of view? Use details from the text to support your answer.

_____
_____
_____
_____
_____
_____
_____

Warm Up 9

Read this passage and then answer the questions that follow.

Paint Pals

1. Paravi and Thuy had been friends since first grade, so naturally they wanted to do their community service projects together.

2. "My brother's teacher said we could volunteer at the preschool next week," Thuy suggested.

3. "It sounds like fun—toddlers are so cute!" gushed Paravi.

4. On Monday, the girls bounced enthusiastically into the Sunny Day Preschool; they were greeted warmly by the school's director, who walked them to the two-year-old classroom.

5. "It'll be a piece of cake," whispered Paravi to Thuy as they marched down the hall, looking official.

6. "Wow, this place brings back memories—snacks, naps, the sandbox," Thuy said, her eyes twinkling.

7. Within moments, Thuy's expectations were fully realized: A group of toddlers was sitting around a table, munching on cheese and crackers; in the adjacent room, little bodies were curled up on cots as soft music played; a few stragglers remained outside playing in the sandbox.

8. "Thanks so much for your assistance," said the teacher. "Are you girls ready for a challenge?"

9. "Sure," they responded in unison, disregarding the precautionary words. Thuy was sent to help coax the tag-alongs into the nap room and was welcomed by three jumping, screaming, very sandy toddlers. Meanwhile, Paravi was instructed to clean the snack table; she was greeted by cracker crumbs crunching underneath her feet and cheese smashed into every crevice in the table.

Warm Up 9 • Paint Pals

10   At art time, Thuy and Paravi put smocks on the children and led them to the easels outside. The girls went back inside to get paintbrushes from the supply room, and were shocked by the disastrous scene they found when they returned: The toddlers had finger-painted their clothing, cheeks, noses, and ears! As the girls devoted the rest of the day to cleanup, they realized this project was much more than they had bargained for.

Warm Up 9 • Paint Pals

Name_____ Date_____

1. This question has two parts. Answer Part A first. Then answer Part B.

   Part A How do the girls' personalities help shape the plot of "Paint Pals"?

   A Their cheerful natures allow them to make it through a terrible day.

   B Their love of children helps them do a great job taking care of the toddlers.

   C Their overconfidence ruins what should have been a fun learning experience.

   D Their inexperience prevents them from knowing what to expect from the toddlers.

   Part B What additional story element helps shape the plot?

   A the setting in a preschool

   B the personality of the teacher

   C the setting during the early afternoon

   D the personalities of the individual children

Question 1

Reread the first few paragraphs of the passage. Think about what these paragraphs tell the reader about the characters Thuy and Paravi. Then ask yourself how this affects what happens later in the story.

continued

Common Core Reading Warm-Ups & Test Practice Grade 7 • ©2014 Newmark Learning, LLC

Warm Up 9 • Paint Pals

Name_____ Date_____

Question 2

Sometimes you can guess the meaning of an unfamiliar word by thinking of a related word whose definition you know. The word *expectations* is related to the verb *expect*. If you know the meaning of *expect*, you can use this information to help you answer the question.

2. Read this sentence from "Paint Pals."

> Within moments, Thuy's <u>expectations</u> were fully realized: A group of toddlers were sitting around a table, munching on cheese and crackers; in the adjacent room, little bodies were curled up on cots as soft music played; a few stragglers remained outside playing in the sandbox.

What does the word <u>expectations</u> mean?

A things a person is worried about

B things a person thinks will happen

C things a person has seen in a dream

D things a person has told others about

Question 3

The point of view of a story is the perspective through which the story is told. It can be a character in the story or an outside narrator who knows the thoughts and feelings of some or all of the characters. A story told from the point of view of a character might begin: I had been waiting for this day for weeks!. A story with an outside narrator might begin: Jess had been waiting for this day for weeks.

3. From whose point of view is the story "Paint Pals" told?

A Thuy and Paravi

B the school's director and teacher

C an outside narrator who knows the thoughts and feelings of all of the characters

D an outside narrator who knows the thoughts and feelings of only some of the characters

52 Warm Up 9

Common Core Reading Warm-Ups & Test Practice Grade 7 • ©2014 Newmark Learning, LLC

Name_____ Date_____

Warm Up 9 • Paint Pals

4. Describe how Paravi and Thuy's point of view about working with toddlers changes from the beginning of the story to the end of the story. Use details from the text to support your answer.

_____
_____
_____
_____
_____
_____

Question 4

To answer this question, you will need to find details that show the characters' points of view. Reread the first part of the story and underline any details in the story that show how Paravi and Thuy view their community service project. Then reread the last section and underline any details that show what the characters think or feel. Use the details you find to write your response.

Warm Up 10

Read this passage and then answer the questions that follow.

Water Safety

1   On a hot summer day, nothing seems as refreshing as a quick dip in a lake or pool. Boating is delightful on a warm, breezy afternoon, and a soak in a hot tub at night can relax aching muscles. Yet each of these activities requires vigilance about water safety.

2   All people, but especially those with small children, should understand the importance of water safety around pools and baths. According to the Red Cross, drowning is the leading cause of accidental death for children younger than five in the United States, and swimming pools are the number one drowning risk for preschoolers. Children can drown in as little as one inch of water, and they usually do not splash or make a sound. For this reason, it is important to establish consistent water safety rules to minimize this risk. The most important rule is to never leave a young child alone near the water for even a second. Even if a child knows how to swim, do not be lulled into thinking he or she is safe if unsupervised.

3   Because adults typically use hot tubs and watercraft, such as jet skis and boats, most people do not consider the dangers they can pose. People have been seriously burned by whirlpools with water that is too hot. In addition, people have had hair entangled in jets in the tubs, which can cause injuries and even drowning. Watercrafts require maturity and skill to handle. Operators and passengers should always wear life jackets when aboard any watercraft and protect their eyes and skin from the harsh sun and water debris.

4   Not enough people realize the importance of water safety; don't be one of them. The next time you are enjoying an activity in or around the water, have fun, but be smart and safe.

Warm Up 10 • Water Safety

Name_____ Date_____

Question 1

Sometimes you can guess the meaning of an unfamiliar word by thinking about the meanings of its parts. The word *refreshing* is made up of the prefix *re-* and the word *fresh*. The meaning of *re-* is "again." How can you put this information together to help you answer the question?

1. Read this sentence from "Water Safety."

> On a hot summer day, nothing seems as refreshing as a quick dip in a lake or pool.

What does the word refreshing mean?

A to lower one's stress

B to restore one's interest

C to renew one's energy

D to lower one's temperature

Question 2

In informational texts, each paragraph might focus on one central idea. Reread the body paragraphs of "Water Safety" and determine the central idea of each.

2. Identify two central ideas from "Water Safety." Check the box next to each statement you choose.

☐ Children can drown in shallow water.

☐ Adults can drown in whirlpools and hot tubs.

☐ Adults must supervise children in water.

☐ Adults must be careful when using certain water devices.

☐ Swimming and boating are pleasant activities.

☐ Adults should protect themselves from sun damage when on the water.

Warm Up 10 • Water Safety

Name_____ Date_____

3. This question has two parts. Answer Part A first. Then answer Part B.

Part A What is the author's argument in paragraph 2 of "Water Safety"?

A Children are safe in water if they know how to swim.

B Children can drown in very shallow pool or bath water.

C Children should not be left alone when they are near or in the water.

D Children should not be allowed in even shallow swimming pools.

Part B Is the information presented in paragraph 2 sufficient to support this argument?

A Yes, because the paragraph describes the author's own experiences with the issue.

B Yes, because the paragraph provides facts and outlines the possible dangers of water.

C No, because the paragraph only provides information about swimming accidents in one type of body of water.

D No, because the paragraph does not take into account the evidence that opposes the author's claims.

Question 3
The strongest expression of an author's argument usually occurs at the end of the section, where the author sums up his points and makes the final statement of his claims. Reread the end of paragraph 2 to help you answer this question.

continued

Warm Up 10 • Water Safety

Name_____ Date_____

Question 4

Reread the passage and underline any statements about boats and jet skis. Review all of the statements together to determine the author's point of view.

4. What is the author's point of view on the use of jet skis and boats? Use details from the text to support your answer.

_____
_____
_____
_____
_____
_____
_____
_____

Practice Test 1

Read the passage. Then answer questions 1–10.

Helping Hands

1. Maya was finishing up her sketch as her friend Trent gazed over her shoulder, his eyes occasionally squinting at her work. Finally, after what seemed like an eternity, Maya gently set her colored pencil down.

2. As part of an art project for their class, Maya and Trent had volunteered to design a mural for the elementary school. For weeks, Maya could think of little else; every time an idea popped into her head, she busily sketched it out. Soon her notebook was bulging with all kinds of images, from bold designs consisting of lines, circles, and squiggles to florals bursting forth in a riot of color.

3. Trent also had worked on a number of designs; he often barricaded himself in the library, where he busily scribbled away. Like Maya, he had made a point of sketching any idea when inspiration struck; but instead of keeping his work in a sketchbook, Trent had a habit of cramming his drawings in his pockets or wherever it seemed handy. He once complained that a lot of his work literally was a wash because his mother was constantly pulling his sketches from the washing machine.

continued

Practice Test 1 • Helping Hands

4   As Maya waited in anticipation for Trent's response to her drawing, she nervously played with a bandanna tied around her backpack. She watched as Trent analyzed her sketch, turning it every which way.

5   "Maya," Trent said cautiously, "this is a great design, but I am not sure this is the best we can do."

6   Maya glared at Trent and said, "Alright, what is your brilliant idea?"

7   Trent, with a genial look, said, "Maya, don't misunderstand—I really like what you created. It's just I think we can do better. Here, let me show you what has been bouncing around in my brain."

8   Trent grabbed his backpack and carefully extracted a rolled-up piece of paper. As he unrolled the paper on top of the desk, he said, "It occurred to me that maybe we don't need to do the mural ourselves; why not let the students at the elementary school help, too?"

9   Maya's annoyance showed Trent what she thought of that idea.

10   "No, really: how about letting all the kids help with the mural?" Trent questioned. "Just look at the sketch—that's all I ask. If you don't like the idea, we can go with yours. I promise."

11   Maya reluctantly glanced at the drawing. Trent had sketched out some of the school's activities: There were students playing instruments in the school band, working in the community garden, and running on the playground. There were even students in an art class, though the teacher looked suspiciously like Trent.

12   "Hmm . . ." said Maya. She then noticed that each activity had a continuous border around it—almost like looking at panels of a comic strip. As she peered more closely, she saw that the border was made up of—hands!

13   "What is with the hands, Trent?" asked an exasperated Maya.

14   "Ah," said Trent enthusiastically, "not just any hands, but student hands. I thought we could let the students put their handprints on the mural. That way it truly will be a mural created by the school. Everybody—students, teachers, even the cafeteria and maintenance workers—can pitch in! What do you think?"

15   Suddenly Maya saw what Trent had envisioned: In her mind she could see small children being helped by the older students as they carefully placed their handprints on the wall. The wall would truly be filled with color and light—and the energy of everyone who helped.

16   Maya looked at an expectant Trent and said, "Well, you can count me in!"

Practice Test 1 • Helping Hands

Name_____ Date_____

1. This question has two parts. Answer Part A first. Then answer Part B.

Part A Which sentence **best** describes a theme of the passage?

A Working together can result in great things.

B It is important to follow through on projects.

C Art can be used to solve problems.

D Successful projects require organized ideas.

Part B Which statement from the passage supports the answer to Part A?

A For weeks, Maya could think of little else; every time an idea popped into her head, she busily sketched it out.

B . . . Trent had a habit of cramming his drawings in his pockets or wherever it seemed handy.

C Maya looked at an expectant Trent and said, "Well, you can count me in!"

D The wall would truly be filled with color and light—and the energy of everyone who helped.

Practice Test 1 • Helping Hands

Name_____ Date_____

2. This question has two parts. Answer Part A first. Then answer Part B.
Read this sentence from the passage.

> She watched as Trent <u>analyzed</u> her sketch, turning it every which way.

Part A What does <u>analyzed</u> mean as it is used in this sentence?

A memorized

B examined

C admired

D criticized

Part B Which phrase from the passage helps you understand the meaning of <u>analyzed</u>?

A can do better

B waited in anticipation

C this is a great design

D turning it every which way

Practice Test 1 • Helping Hands

Name_____ Date_____

3. What evidence from the passage supports the idea that Maya cares about what Trent thinks of her mural design?

A   Maya reluctantly glanced at the drawing.

B   Maya's annoyance showed Trent what she thought of that idea.

C   For weeks, Maya could think of little else; every time an idea popped into her head, she busily sketched it out.

D   As Maya waited in anticipation for Trent's response to her drawing, she nervously played with a bandanna tied around her backpack.

4. Decide which statements belong in a summary of the story. Then number them in the correct order.

___   Maya reluctantly looked at Trent's design and listened to his idea.

___   Trent's sketches of mural designs went through the washing machine.

___   They spent weeks sketching mural ideas, trying to plan the perfect design.

___   Maya and Trent volunteered to design a mural for a wall at the elementary school.

___   Maya noticed that the borders on Trent's design were made of handprints.

___   Maya agreed to Trent's plan once she understood it.

___   When Maya showed Trent her design, he said he liked it but they could do better.

5. Read this sentence from the passage.

> Like Maya, he had made a point of sketching any idea when inspiration struck; but instead of keeping his work in a sketchbook, Trent had a habit of cramming his drawings in his pockets or wherever it seemed handy.

Which word means the same as cramming, as it is used in this sentence?

A scribbling

B creating

C stuffing

D laying

6. How does each character contribute to the story's resolution?

A Trent excitedly explains the handprint border and Maya finally understands the purpose of his mural.

B Maya gets tired of arguing with Trent and agrees to use his mural sketch.

C Trent patiently asks Maya questions about her sketch until she realizes her mural will not work.

D Trent describes his sketch and Maya realizes he is passionate about his idea.

Practice Test 1 • Helping Hands

Name_____ Date_____

7. Based on the information in the story, decide whether each word describes Maya or Trent. Write each word in the correct column. If a word describes both, write it in both columns.

| Artistic | Creative | Honest | Organized | Disorganized |

Maya	Trent

Practice Test 1 • Helping Hands

Name_____ Date_____

8. What is Maya's reaction to Trent's mural idea and how does this reaction affect the plot? Use details from the text to support your answer.

_____
_____
_____
_____
_____
_____
_____

9. Identify the conflict and the theme of the story. How does the conflict help readers understand the theme? Use details from the text to support your answer.

_____
_____
_____
_____
_____
_____
_____

continued

Practice Test 1 • Helping Hands

Name_____ Date_____

10. Maya and Trent have different ideas about the mural project. How are their ideas alike? How are they different? Use details from the text to support your answer.

_____

_____

_____

_____

_____

_____

_____

_____

_____

_____

_____

_____

_____

Practice Test 2

Read the passage. Then answer questions 1–10.

from *The Story of the Pony Express*

Operation, Equipment, and Business

1   The riders dressed as they saw fit. The average costume consisted of a buckskin shirt, ordinary trousers tucked into high leather boots, and a slouch hat or cap. They always went armed. At first a Spencer carbine was carried strapped to the rider's back, besides a sheath knife at his side. In the saddle holsters he carried a pair of Colt's revolvers. After a time the carbines were left off and only side arms taken along. The carrying of larger guns meant extra weight, and it was made a rule of the Company that a rider should never fight unless compelled to do so. He was to depend wholly upon speed for safety. The record of the service fully justified this policy.

continued

Practice Test 2 • from *The Story of the Pony Express*

2   While the horses were of the highest grade, they were of mixed breed and were purchased over a wide range of territory. Good results were obtained from blooded animals from the Missouri Valley, but considerable preference was shown for the western-bred mustangs. These animals were about fourteen hands high and averaged less than 900 pounds in weight. A former blacksmith for the Company who was at one time located at Seneca, Kansas, recalls that one of these native ponies often had to be thrown and staked down with a rope tied to each foot before it could be shod. Then, before the smith could pare the hoofs and nail on the shoes, it was necessary for one man to sit astride the animal's head, and another on its body, while the beast continued to struggle and squeal. To shoe one of these animals often required a half day of strenuous work.

3   As might be expected, the horse as well as rider traveled very light. The combined weight of the saddle, bridle, and saddlebags did not exceed thirteen pounds. The saddle-bag used by the pony rider for carrying mail was called a *mochila*; it had openings in the center so it would fit snugly over the horn and tree of the saddle and yet be removable without delay.

4   The mochila had four pockets called *cantinas* in each of its corners—one in front and one behind each of the rider's legs. These cantinas held the mail. All were kept carefully locked and three were opened en route only at military posts—Forts Kearney, Laramie, Bridger, Churchill, and at Salt Lake City. The fourth pocket was for the local or way mail-stations. Each local station-keeper had a key and could open it when necessary. It held a time-card on which a record of the arrival and departure at the various stations where it was opened, was kept. Only one mochila was used on a trip; it was transferred by the rider from one horse to another until the destination was reached.

Practice Test 2 • from *The Story of the Pony Express*

5   Letters were wrapped in oil silk to protect them from moisture, either from stormy weather, fording streams, or perspiring animals. While a mail of twenty pounds might be carried, the average weight did not exceed fifteen pounds. The postal charges were at first, five dollars for each half-ounce letter, but this rate was afterward reduced by the Post Office Department to one dollar for each half ounce. At this figure it remained as long as the line was in business. In addition to this rate, a regulation government envelope costing ten cents had to be purchased. Patrons generally made use of an especially light tissue paper for their correspondence. The large newspapers of New York, Boston, Chicago, St. Louis, and San Francisco were among the best customers of the service.

Practice Test 2 • from *The Story of the Pony Express*

Name_____ Date_____

1. Which statement would be included in a summary of the passage?

A Pony Express riders should have worn uniforms.

B Pony Express riders were always armed.

C The Pony Express used mixed-breed horses.

D Riders tucked their pants into their high leather boots.

2. This question has two parts. Answer Part A first. Then answer Part B.

Part A Read this sentence from the passage:

> The combined weight of the saddle, bridle, and saddlebags did not <u>exceed</u> thirteen pounds.

What is the meaning of <u>exceed</u> as it is used in this sentence?

A to estimate

B to be of high quality

C to display the contents of

D to go beyond a quantity or rate

Part B Which phrase from the passage helps you understand the meaning of <u>exceed</u>?

A traveled very light

B were of the highest grade

C depend wholly upon speed

D this rate was afterward reduced

Practice Test 2

72

3. This question has two parts. Answer Part A first. Then answer Part B.

Part A Why did people write letters on light tissue paper?

A It dried quickly when the mail got wet.

B The cost of sending mail was based on weight.

C It was the only kind of paper available at the military posts.

D Ink showed up better on tissue paper than standard paper.

Part B Which sentence from paragraph 5 supports the answer to Part A?

A Letters were wrapped in oil silk to protect them from moisture, either from stormy weather, fording streams, or perspiring animals.

B While a mail of twenty pounds might be carried, the average weight did not exceed fifteen pounds.

C The postal charges were at first, five dollars for each half-ounce letter, but this rate was afterward reduced by the Post Office Department to one dollar for each half ounce.

D In addition to this rate, a regulation government envelope costing ten cents had to be purchased.

Practice Test 2 • from *The Story of the Pony Express*

Name_____ Date_____

4. Which statements correctly describe a mochila, according to the passage? Check the box next to each answer you choose.

☐ A mochila was a saddlebag used to carry mail.

☐ Openings in the center allowed it to fit on the saddle.

☐ It had six mail pockets called cantinas.

☐ A mochila had pockets that locked.

☐ Three pockets were only opened at military posts.

☐ Each horse on the route had its own mochila.

5. Choose three details from the passage that support the idea that the horses and riders carried as little weight as possible. Check the box next to each detail you choose.

☐ The carrying of larger guns meant extra weight, and it was made a rule of the Company that a rider should never fight unless compelled to do so.

☐ The combined weight of the saddle, bridle, and saddlebags did not exceed thirteen pounds.

☐ Letters were wrapped in oil silk to protect them from moisture, either from stormy weather, fording streams, or perspiring animals.

☐ While a mail of twenty pounds might be carried, the average weight did not exceed fifteen pounds.

☐ These animals were about fourteen hands high and averaged less than 900 pounds in weight.

☐ The postal charges were at first, five dollars for each half-ounce letter, but this rate was afterward reduced by the Post Office Department to one dollar for each half ounce.

6. Choose two statements that describe the text structure in the passage and how the author develops ideas. Check the box next to each statement you choose.

☐ The author organizes information in chronological order.

☐ Each paragraph describes a different safety measure taken by the Pony Express Company.

☐ Each paragraph describes a different Pony Express topic.

☐ The author describes the effects of the Pony Express.

☐ The author organizes information according to geographic location.

☐ All the information provided in the passage relates back to the chapter title.

☐ A different piece of equipment used by riders is described in each paragraph.

continued

Practice Test 2 • from *The Story of the Pony Express*

Name_____ Date_____

7. Which details from the text support the inference that the horses were strong, powerful animals? Place a check before each detail you choose.

☐ Then, before the smith could pare the hoofs and nail on the shoes, it was necessary for one man to sit astride the animal's head, and another on its body, while the beast continued to struggle and squeal.

☐ While the horses were of the highest grade, they were of mixed breed and were purchased over a wide range of territory.

☐ As might be expected, the horse as well as rider traveled very light.

☐ A former blacksmith for the Company who was at one time located at Seneca, Kansas, recalls that one of these native ponies often had to be thrown and staked down with a rope tied to each foot before it could be shod.

☐ Only one mochila was used on a trip; it was transferred by the rider from one horse to another until the destination was reached.

☐ To shoe one of these animals often required a half day of strenuous work.

☐ Good results were obtained from blooded animals from the Missouri Valley, but considerable preference was shown for the western-bred mustangs.

Practice Test 2 • from *The Story of the Pony Express*

8. What is the author's purpose in writing this passage? Use at least two details from the text to support your answer.

___

9. According to the passage, Pony Express riders "always went armed." Does the author provide relevant evidence to support this statement? Use two or more details from the text to support your answer.

___

continued

Practice Test 2 • from *The Story of the Pony Express*

Name_____ Date_____

10. Identify two central ideas and explain how they are developed over the course of the passage. Use details from the passage to support your answer.

_____

_____

_____

_____

_____

_____

_____

_____

_____

_____

_____

_____

_____

Practice Test 3

Read the passages. Then answer questions 1–10.

The Land of the Free

1   Outside, the streets are alive with people walking, flags waving, and colorfully decorated cars driving slowly in a parade. A band playing the national anthem marches through the intersection, their brass instruments glimmering in the sun. I can hear and smell the sizzle of hot dogs and hamburgers cooking on backyard barbecues. The warm summer air sifts through the red, white, and blue streamers hanging from unlit streetlights.

2   "Hey, Cooper," a familiar voice calls out. "Over here—give me a hand!"

3   I peek around the shoulders of a man in an Uncle Sam costume and see my friend Shelly standing next to a stationary float on the side of the road. With a sideways shuffle and a few apologies, I work through the crowd and across the street to meet Shelly.

4   She grasps me by the shoulders and pulls me in for an uncharacteristically solemn chat. "Tell me you can fix a flat tire," she says.

5   It's hard to take her seriously when she's pointing to a trailer decorated like a watermelon. It's a tradition in my neighborhood to hold the watermelon-eating contest, and this year, having devoured thirteen slices, Shelly won. Now she's wearing a green dress, a tiara, and a stain of pink juice around her downturned mouth.

continued

Practice Test 3 • The Land of the Free • Fireworks

6   I shrug my shoulders and say, "Sorry, Shelly, I wish I did."

7   As soon as the words are out of my mouth, she deflates like the airless tire beside her. Although everyone agrees that Watermelon Queen is sort of a silly contest, it's obvious that Shelly is more than a little displeased with the current situation. We watch helplessly as the parade rattles on in a commotion of jubilant music and laughter.

8   Down the road I see dozens of men and women marching in formation, their feet pounding the pavement with perfect precision. As they come closer, I realize they're all wearing military uniforms from different decades. A young lieutenant with close-cropped blond hair walks alongside an older veteran who served in the army years ago. The rows advance in harmony, and the rhythmic sound of footsteps creates a unique sound, like a lone drummer beating in time.

9   Then, without a word, several troops break formation as they reach Shelly's float. With the accuracy of a speedway pit crew, they jack up the float, remove the tire, and replace it with a new one. Once the float is safely on the ground, they rejoin the group of soldiers as if nothing had slowed their steady advance.

10   Someone in the crowd yells, "Thank you," though they're not talking about simply changing a tire. Another person starts clapping while someone else lets out a wild whoop. In a moment, everyone is cheering louder than I've ever heard—louder than at football games or after one of the mayor's speeches. We yell and applaud until our throats are sore and our hands are weary, thanking the heroes who made this nation great and who give us a reason to celebrate our freedom.

Fireworks

1 We sit together on blankets beneath the darkened sky,
  And watch and wait and anticipate the first firework to fly.
  The landscape all around us seems motionless until
  A single shadowy figure comes marching 'cross the hill.

5 The moment we've been counting down has finally arrived:
  The ending celebration of this year's Fourth of July.
  Our frankfurters are eaten and the watermelon's gone,
  And streamers from today's parade are lying on the lawn.

  We see a spark ignite and travel up the burning fuse
10 Against the backdrop of the nighttime purple hues.
  A trail of light streaks upward in a crimson-quickened pace
  Like a shooting star set to join its siblings up in space.

The firework ignites in a shimmering silver ball
Casting shadows across the awestruck faces of us all.
15 A loud boom echoes afterward, loud and deep and long
And for whatever reason I start thinking of a song.

It was written by a man named Key centuries ago
When rockets flew across the sky and bombs blew up below.
But still he saw a glimpse of hope standing straight and true:
20 A flag waving in the wind—red and white and blue.

"The Star-Spangled Banner" became the anthem of the free,
Symbolizing the American dream for hope and liberty.
I thought it was just tradition but I've never realized why
This is the reason we have fireworks on the Fourth of July.

1. This question has two parts. Answer Part A first. Then answer Part B.

Part A Why is Shelly unhappy at the beginning of the story?

A because Cooper won't help her

B because her face is pink from eating watermelon

C because her float has a flat tire

D because she is missing the parade

Part B Which sentence from the story provides support for the answer to Part A?

A She grasps me by the shoulders and pulls me in for an uncharacteristically solemn chat. "Tell me you can fix a flat tire," she says.

B Now she's wearing a green dress, a tiara, and a stain of pink juice around her downturned mouth.

C I shrug my shoulders and say, "Sorry, Shelly, I wish I did."

D We watch helplessly as the parade rattles on in a commotion of jubilant music and laughter.

continued

Practice Test 3 • The Land of the Free • Fireworks

Name_____ Date_____

2. Decide which four statements in the chart belong in a summary of the story, and number them in the order in which they occurred.

___ People in the crowd applaud the soldiers for their service to their country.

___ It is a warm summer day and people are celebrating the Fourth of July.

___ Soldiers marching by break formation and fix the flat tire on Shelly's float.

___ Shelly is wearing a green dress and tiara because she won the watermelon-eating contest.

___ Shelly watches the parade with Cooper but cannot participate.

___ Shelly asks Cooper to help her change the flat tire on her parade float.

___ Cooper hears a marching band playing.

___ The soldiers are wearing uniforms from different decades.

___ The soldiers are able to change the tire very quickly.

___ People are barbecuing in their backyards.

3. Read this line from "The Land of the Free."

> As soon as the words are out of my mouth, she deflates like the airless tire beside her.

What does this line reveal about how Shelly feels?

A That she is angry at Cooper.

B That she is disappointed that Cooper cannot help her.

C That she is tired after a long day.

D That she does not want to fix the float.

Name_____ Date_____

4. This question has two parts. Answer Part A first. Then answer Part B.

Part A What is the setting of "Fireworks"?

A the morning before a Fourth of July picnic

B the evening at the end of a Fourth of July celebration

C the day of a Fourth of July party at the beach

D the day after the Fourth of July

Part B Which lines from the poem **best** support the answer to Part A?

A We sit together on blankets beneath the darkened sky, / And watch and wait and anticipate the first firework to fly.

B The landscape all around us seems motionless until / A single shadowy figure comes marching 'cross the hill.

C Our frankfurters are eaten and the watermelon's gone, / And streamers from today's parade are lying on the lawn.

D "The Star-Spangled Banner" became the anthem of the free, / Symbolizing the American dream for hope and liberty.

continued

5. Read these lines from the poem "Fireworks."

> A trail of light streaks upward in a crimson-quickened pace /
> Like a shooting star set to join its siblings up in space.

What does the phrase siblings up in space refer to?

- **A** the stars in the sky
- **B** the fireworks being ignited
- **C** the light caused by the fireworks
- **D** the trail of light left by the fireworks

6. Which word **best** describes the mood created by the language in the poem "Fireworks"?

- **A** awed
- **B** relaxed
- **C** excited
- **D** nervous

Name_____ Date_____

7. Read each statement and decide whether it applies to "The Land of the Free" or "Fireworks." Put a check mark in the correct box beside each piece of information. If the information is included in both passages, put check marks in both boxes.

Information	The Land of the Free	Fireworks
The action takes place on the Fourth of July.	☐	☐
It includes dialogue.	☐	☐
The setting is a picnic.	☐	☐
It has a first-person narrator.	☐	☐
A central theme is patriotism.	☐	☐
A character is disappointed.	☐	☐
The people honor soldiers for serving the country.	☐	☐

continued

Practice Test 3 • The Land of the Free • Fireworks

Name_____ Date_____

8. Describe how Shelly and Cooper feel at the beginning of "The Land of the Free" and how they feel at the end. What causes this change? Use details from the story to support your answer.

_____

_____

_____

_____

_____

_____

_____

Name_____ Date_____

9. At the end of the poem, what realization does the narrator of "Fireworks" have about the tradition of lighting fireworks on the Fourth of July? Use details from the poem to support your answer.

_____

_____

_____

_____

_____

_____

_____

continued

Practice Test 3 • The Land of the Free • Fireworks

Name_____ Date_____

10. Compare and contrast the experiences of the narrators of "The Land of the Free" and "Fireworks." Think about how each narrator feels at the end of the passage. Use details from both selections to support your answer.

Practice Test 4

Read the passages. Then answer questions 1–10.

The Story of Today's Olympics

1   Every four summers and every four winters, the world's most elite athletes gather in one city to compete in the Olympic Games. The Olympics is an international competition that draws the attention of people from almost every region of the planet. From skiing to ice hockey to diving and beach volleyball, every event includes contenders from several nations. In the Summer Olympics of 2012, more than 200 countries were represented. Each nation's citizens always watch eagerly, waving their flag and singing their own national anthem when one of their athletes is victorious in an event. Most of these athletes have labored their whole lives to reach this point.

2   Today's Olympics were inspired by athletic events in ancient Greece. Back in eighth century B.C.E., athletes from different parts of Greece participated in running, horse racing, and fighting competitions. Winning athletes were awarded a crown made of olive leaves, and a sculpture was created in their honor. Written records from ancient Greece include descriptions of the games and the outstanding achievements of the athletes. This Greek tradition of athletic events, which most popularly took place in the city of Olympia—from which the name "Olympics" is derived—continued for about a thousand years.

continued

3   It wasn't until approximately 1,500 years after the ancient Greek tradition had ended that Europeans began talking about reinstating something like it. The idea came from a Frenchman and a group of people who were enthusiastic about his dream. Together they brainstormed ways to organize a worldwide sports competition. Within five or six years of contacting world leaders and promoting the idea, the group had convinced many countries to participate in the Olympics. In 1896, the first-ever international Olympic Games were held in Greece, right where it all began many centuries before. Since then, the games have been held in many cities worldwide. It is considered a great honor for a country and city to be selected to host the games.

4   The modern Olympics began simply: there were no massive stadiums, and at first not many nations joined. But with each four-year leap, the event grew in popularity and athletic prestige. By the early 1900s, the Olympics hosted elite athletes from an increasing number of countries. New technology and improvements in transportation allowed more and more women and men to join the excitement as both competitors and spectators.

5   Today, making it to the Olympics is a dream and goal for many competitive athletes. Olympic athletes can become famous around the world after winning Olympic medals. The games are also a beloved television production that spectators are able to watch from home. Perhaps most importantly, the Olympics Games are a symbol of connection and peace among the countries of our world. Every four years, people across the globe have an opportunity to applaud athletes from places they have never visited, learning stories about and being inspired by those who work hard to achieve great things. As the games become increasingly accessible to viewers, the inspiration continues, promoting peace and athletic determination everywhere.

Big Changes Since Ancient Greece

1   The modern Olympic Games are a long-lived tradition based on sports competitions that began in ancient Greece more than 2,000 years ago. But although ancient Greek athletics inspired today's events, I argue that there are even more differences than similarities between the modern Olympics and the ancient tradition from which the idea came.

2   To begin with, in the Greek games, only men competed; women were not permitted to play sports back then. Even at the late-nineteenth-century genesis of the modern Olympics, women were not nearly as well represented as they are today. Now women participate as men do. In recent decades, there are many sports—such as gymnastics, volleyball, and figure skating—in which the female athletes get far more attention than their male counterparts. This is a significant shift from the world of ancient Greece.

continued

3   Another difference is found from comparing who attended the games. In ancient Greece, mostly locals watched and competed. In stark contrast, people worldwide are part of modern Olympic events. Modern modes of transportation, such as cars, trains, and planes, make travel much easier now than it was in ancient Greece, so many more spectators and athletes attend the games. In fact, the greatest appeal of today's Olympics is its multinational involvement, whereas the ancient event sought mostly to attract nearby citizens of the Greco-Roman empire.

4   Those original games involved far more danger. The events, which were marked by great intensity and little regard for safety measures, included extreme sorts of fighting, as well as horse and foot racing. But today's events are strictly regulated in order to keep athletes safe. Although sports competitions can always be dangerous, competing in the ancient games was drastically more life threatening for athletes. Were they tougher or stronger? Perhaps, but I'd be surprised if that were the case. Today's competitors can do multiple flips in the air, run miles and miles at grueling speeds, and execute strategic team victories; they have plenty of athletic rigor to show for themselves.

5   Furthermore, today there are many sports in the Olympics—almost too many to count. While there were few options for sports in ancient Greece, there are now so many that the Olympics are divided into summer and winter games. And it takes weeks to fit in every event.

6   Lastly, in Greece, the tradition lasted almost a thousand years, while the modern Olympic tradition started in 1896, less than fifteen decades ago. Who knows how the Olympics will change if the modern games continue as long as the ancient Greek ones did? Sports are often being added or removed according to international relevance; there were once events like motorboating and pigeon shooting, but now newer sports like synchronized swimming and speed skating have moved to the forefront. It's hard to even imagine what exciting new sports might exist in the future.

Practice Test 4 • The Story of Today's Olympics • Big Changes Since Ancient Greece

Name_____ Date_____

1. This question has two parts. Answer Part A first. Then answer Part B.

Part A What is the main idea of "The Story of Today's Olympics"?

A Olympic athletes train their entire lives to compete in the Olympic Games.

B The modern Olympics began small in 1896 and have grown into a large international event.

C Although there are many differences, the modern Olympics are based on an ancient Greek tradition.

D The Olympics are held every four summers and every four winters.

Part B Which sentence from the passage **best** supports the answer to question Part A?

A The Olympics is an international competition that draws the attention of people from almost every region of the planet.

B It wasn't until approximately 1,500 years after the ancient Greek tradition had ended that Europeans began talking about reinstating something like it.

C By the early 1900s, elite athletes from an increasing number of countries were participating in the Olympics.

D Today, making it to the Olympics is a dream and goal for many competitive athletes.

continued

2. Based on the information in the passage, which statement **best** describes what caused the Olympic Games to grow in size since being reinstated?

A   Organizers built bigger stadiums to hold the games.

B   Technology and transportation improvements allow more people to watch the Olympics and to participate in the games.

C   It is the goal of many elite athletes to participate in the Olympics.

D   More than 200 countries participated in the most recent Olympics.

Practice Test 4 • The Story of Today's Olympics • Big Changes Since Ancient Greece

Name_____ Date_____

3. This question has two parts. Answer Part A first. Then answer Part B.

Part A What is the author's main purpose in "Big Changes Since Ancient Greece"?

A to persuade the reader that there are more differences than similarities between the original Olympics and the modern Olympics

B to inform the reader about how the Olympic Games have changed over the past century

C to entertain the reader with a story about the athletes that competed in the ancient Olympic Games

D to encourage the reader to learn more about how the Olympics have changed since the times of the ancient Greeks

Part B Which sentence from the passage **best** supports the answer to Part A?

A But although ancient Greek athletics inspired today's events, I argue that there are even more differences than similarities between the modern Olympics and the ancient tradition from which the idea came.

B To begin with, in the Greek games, only men competed; women were not permitted to play sports back then.

C The events, which were marked by great intensity and little regard for safety measures, included extreme sorts of fighting, as well as horse and foot racing.

D Sports are often being added or removed according to international relevance; there were once events like motorboating and pigeon shooting, but now newer sports like synchronized swimming and speed skating have moved to the forefront.

continued

Practice Test 4 • The Story of Today's Olympics • Big Changes Since Ancient Greece

Name_____ Date_____

4. Read this sentence from paragraph 4 of "Big Changes Since Ancient Greece."

> Today's competitors can do multiple flips in the air, run miles and miles at grueling speeds, and execute <u>strategic</u> team victories; they have plenty of athletic rigor to show for themselves.

Which word or phrase means about the same as <u>strategic</u>?

A   long-term

B   extremely difficult

C   carefully planned

D   unlikely

5. Read the following sentence from the passage.

> In fact, the greatest appeal of today's Olympics is its <u>multinational involvement</u>, whereas the ancient event sought mostly to attract nearby citizens of the Greco-Roman empire.

What does the phrase <u>multinational involvement</u> refer to in this sentence?

A   the participation of many different countries

B   the large number of athletes who compete

C   the spectators who watch from around the world

D   the Greco-Roman citizens who attended the ancient games

Practice Test 4 • The Story of Today's Olympics • Big Changes Since Ancient Greece

Name_____ Date_____

6. Read each piece of information in the chart. Decide whether the detail describes the Olympic Games of the ancient Greeks or modern Olympic Games based on the information in "Big Changes Since Ancient Greece" and "The Story of Today's Olympics." Put a check mark in the correct box beside each piece of information. If the information describes both the games of the ancient Greeks and modern Olympics, put check marks in both boxes.

Information	Ancient Olympics	Modern Olympics
Popular events include women's gymnastics and figure skating.	☐	☐
People around the world are spectators.	☐	☐
Extreme fighting is included as an event.	☐	☐
The achievements of the athletes are respected and admired.	☐	☐
Games are divided into winter and summer events.	☐	☐
Athletes come only from nearby.	☐	☐
Pigeon shooting is included as an event.	☐	☐

continued

Practice Test 4 • The Story of Today's Olympics • Big Changes Since Ancient Greece

Name_____ Date_____

7. Read each piece of information in the chart. Decide whether the information is included in "The Story of Today's Olympics" or "Big Changes Since Ancient Greece." Put a check mark in the correct box beside each piece of information. If the information is included in both passages, put check marks in both boxes.

Information	The Story of Today's Olympics	Big Changes Since Ancient Greece
The Olympic Games are held every four summers and every four winters.	☐	☐
Athletes come from all over the world to compete in the Olympic Games.	☐	☐
The modern Olympics were first held in Greece.	☐	☐
The idea for the modern Olympic Games came from a Frenchman.	☐	☐
The games of ancient Greece could be life threatening for the athletes.	☐	☐
The modern Olympics were inspired by games held in ancient Greece.	☐	☐
The Olympic Games are named after the Greek city of Olympia.	☐	☐
Modern Olympic athletes may well be tougher and stronger than the athletes in ancient Greece.	☐	☐
There were only a few events in the ancient Greek games.	☐	☐

8. Read this sentence from the last paragraph.

> Perhaps most importantly, the Olympics Games are a symbol of connection and peace among the countries of our world.

How does the author support the opinion that the Olympic Games are a symbol of connection and peace? Use details from "The Story of Today's Olympics" to support your answer.

_____
_____
_____
_____
_____
_____

9. Describe how the events that modern athletes compete in are different from those that took place in the Olympic Games of ancient Greece. Use details from both "The Story of Today's Olympics" and "Big Changes Since Ancient Greece" to support your answer.

_____
_____
_____
_____
_____
_____

continued

Practice Test 4 • The Story of Today's Olympics • Big Changes Since Ancient Greece

Name_____ Date_____

10. Compare and contrast the author's purpose in the passage "The Story of Today's Olympics" with the author's purpose in the passage "Big Changes Since Ancient Greece." Include details from both passages to support your answer.

_____

_____

_____

_____

_____

_____

_____

_____

_____

_____

_____

_____

_____

_____